# Rosalind Kerven

# The Ogre's Guitar

*Illustrated by* **Peter Gray**

# The Pooka and the Piper

*Illustrated by* **Brian Lee**

**OXFORD**
UNIVERSITY PRESS

# Contents

# The Ogre's Guitar

*A Caribbean folk tale*

No one knew where the ogre came from.
He flew to the island on the back of a
storm. He covered the land in darkness.
He spat out whirlwinds and hailstones.
He beat the people into sleep and filled
their dreams with evil shadows.

The ogre cursed, and cackled with laughter.
He crept to a secret hole, deep in the heart
of the island. There he set to work, casting
his evil spells.

At long last, the storm died down and all the people woke up. They stumbled to their doors, peered outside – and screamed! For everything – yes, *everything* – was covered by forest.

There were trees everywhere, towering to the sky. Their trunks were crusty and their branches were twisted and tangled into weird shapes. Their sickly, green leaves oozed sticky sap.

Everything else had vanished. There were no yards or gardens, no paths or gates, no tracks or roads. There was no way out of the forest. Everyone was trapped!

Time passed. Every day, all over the island, brave men tried to fight their way through the forest. They were all big, strong men, and they armed themselves with knives and axes.

But none of them ever came back or were ever seen again. They had all been eaten by the ogre!

Right in the middle of the island there lived an old woman who had twenty-two grandchildren, all of them boys. Her oldest grandsons had already gone out, one by one, to try to break through the forest. Every one of them had disappeared.

Now only the youngest two were left. These two boys were called Taywo and Kayinday. They were not ordinary boys. They were special – they were twins.

Taywo and Kayinday said to their grandmother, "It's our turn to go out into the forest today. We want to try our luck."

Tears rolled down the old woman's cheeks. She was afraid she would never see them again. But she didn't try to stop them. Instead, she went and called the boys' grandfather.

Now, this old man was an *obeah*, a wise man. Long ago he had lived in Africa, and had learned many secret things.

Grandfather led Taywo and Kayinday to a wooden chest. He opened the lid and pulled out two strange necklaces. They were both made of black pearls and ebony.

The old man said, "Sadly, there was nothing I could do for your older brothers when they went out into the forest. These necklaces can only be worn by twins, like you."

He slipped the necklaces over the boys' heads.

"Always wear these on your journey," he told them. "They are magic, and will help you."

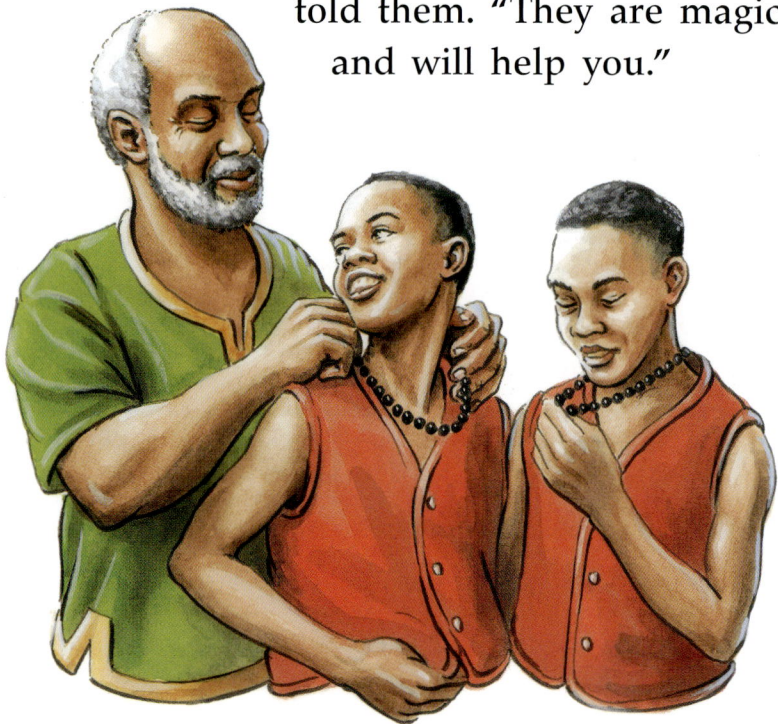

Taywo and Kayinday thanked their grandfather. Then they went out into the forest. They didn't take knives or axes with them: they just took their necklaces.

As they walked, the necklaces caught the shafts of sunlight falling through the thick leaves. By magic, the trees parted and made a path! The boys followed this path for seven days. They saw nothing, and nothing happened.

So they walked on and on, down the magic path for yet another seven days. And then suddenly, they could walk no further. Something huge, something terrifying, was blocking the way.

Yes! It was the ogre!

He was horribly ugly. His face was square:
part of it was blood red, and part of it was
white like death. His mouth was a slash
that stretched from ear to ear, with filthy
teeth hanging out of it. His eyes bulged
like a frog's. His nose was an empty hole.
He was covered in slimy scales.

The ogre was lying there, fast asleep, and
his bed was made of human bones.

Kayinday hid behind some trees while Taywo crept towards the ogre. When he was close, Taywo broke a branch off a tree and tickled the ogre's nose with the leaves.

The ogre woke up. He yawned and stretched and snorted. Then his eyes fell on Taywo.

"You boy," he hissed, "what do you want?"

"I only want to walk past you, sir," Taywo replied politely.

The ogre's mouth twisted into a nasty smile.

"Of course you can, young friend," he cackled. "But you'll have to do something for me first."

The ogre felt under his pile of bones and pulled something out. It was a guitar – a fantastic shiny guitar, cut into a crazy shape and painted with dazzling colours.

"Take this!" demanded the ogre.

Taywo took it.

"Play it!" urged the ogre. "Play the guitar so that I can dance to it. If you can play for longer than I can dance, then I'll let you pass. But if you dare to stop playing before I'm tired, then I shall gobble you right up!"

Taywo took the guitar and started to play. The ogre grinned. Then he began jigging and hopping and spinning about. Taywo played and the ogre danced non-stop for four long hours. The ogre wasn't tired at all, but Taywo's fingers were sore and bleeding.

"Please sir," he gasped, "can I go and get a drink from the river behind that tree?"

Before the ogre had time to reply, Taywo had darted behind the tree where Kayinday was hiding. At once, Kayinday leaped out. He ran over, picked up the guitar and began to play. The ogre didn't realize that Kayinday had taken Taywo's place because the twins looked exactly the same.

Kayinday played for another four hours until he was worn out, too. Then he and Taywo secretly changed places again. All the time, the ogre kept on dancing.

Taywo played for another four hours until he was tired again; and then Kayinday came back and took his place. All the time, the ogre kept on dancing.

The two boys kept taking turns to play the guitar, while the ogre danced non-stop. They went on and on, all through the day and the night and the next day. But at long last, something strange began to happen to the ogre.

His whole body grew red hot. His scaly skin bubbled and foamed. Flames shot from his frog-eyes and his slash-mouth. Smoke poured from the dark hole of his nose. He was on fire!

Still the twins kept on playing the guitar. Still the bubbling, flaming, smoking ogre kept on dancing. Then all at once there was a dazzling FLASH and a loud CRASH! The ogre fell down. He had danced himself to death!

Kayinday dropped the guitar. Taywo crept out from behind the tree where he was hiding. They stared at the dead ogre. Then they whooped with joy and hugged each other. But the next minute they had a terrible fright. They heard strange voices, calling them. The boys couldn't see where the voices came from, and yet they were very near.

"Taywo! Kayinday!" called the voices. "Well done! Now bury the ogre in the dark, deep ground."

The boys looked around. There was nobody else there, only the dead body of the ogre. Then suddenly, the boys realized where the voices came from. Their magic necklaces were speaking to them!

The twins dug a deep hole. They threw the ogre's body into it, and covered it with black earth. As the ogre's body disappeared from sight, amazing things began to happen.

All over the island, the tangled trees crumbled away into dust. Then the ogre's bed of human bones suddenly came to life! The bones turned into all the lost men who had died trying to break through the tangled forest – including Taywo and Kayinday's twenty older brothers.

The evil spell was broken!

# The Pooka and the Piper

*An Irish folk tale*

Everyone used to say that Shane O'Toole was useless. He couldn't be bothered to do his school work, his writing was a mess, and he was always getting into trouble. Shane was interested in only one thing – making music. But it wasn't pop music, or classical or jazz that he liked. No, our Shane was crazy about the bagpipes.

Shane had an old set of pipes that he'd bought at a jumble sale, but no one would teach him how to play them . . . until the night of his big adventure!

One evening, Shane was sitting by the bridge near his house, trying to get a tune out of his pipes. Suddenly, something came up and butted him hard on the backside! He spun round. A huge animal was standing there. It was like a horse with goat's horns, and it had a twisted, grinning mouth.

The animal stepped back and butted Shane again, tossing him high up into the air. Shane screamed, then fell – not to the ground, but onto the animal's back. Then the animal went galloping away with him, carrying him into the night.

After a while, the animal stopped and turned its head to look at Shane. Then it opened its mouth and spoke.

"Do you know what I am, Shane?" it asked.

Shane's teeth were chattering loudly, but he managed to answer, "N . . . no."

"I'm a pooka," said the animal. "Can you guess where I'm taking you?"

"N . . . no," replied Shane.

"To the house of the banshees," said the pooka.

"Wh . . . what are banshees?" whispered Shane.

The pooka gave a shriek of laughter. "The banshees? What, don't you know them, Shane? They're the wailing ladies of death!"

The pooka galloped on and on through the night. It carried Shane over windy hills and misty marshes. At last, they reached the top of a high mountain. There was a big rock there, and the pooka kicked it hard with its hoof three times.

At once, a door slid open in the rock, and a bright light shone out. The pooka neighed like a horse. Then it carried Shane inside.

"You can get down now," said the pooka.

So Shane slid off the pooka's back, and followed it down a long passage towards the light.

Very soon they came to a big room with candles hanging all around the walls. There seemed to be a party going on. A long, golden table stood in the middle of the room. It was covered with dishes full of delicious food and jugs of sparkling drink. All around the table stood the banshees.

They were all old hags, hundreds of them, very tall and bony. Their straggly, grey hair was matted with cobwebs. Their dresses were pale and brittle, and they had sunken, wrinkled faces. Yet, as they walked about, some of them were lit by sudden flashes of beauty.

The pooka neighed again. At once, all the banshees turned round to look at it.

"Ladies!" cried the pooka. "Just look at who I've brought you. This handsome young lad here is called Shane, and he's come to play the pipes for you!"

"No, no" cried Shane. "This is a mistake! I can't really play anything. Anyway, I've left my bagpipes back at the bridge . . ."

But before he could finish, one of the banshees stamped hard on the floor, and a door in the wall swung open. An enormous goose flew out, carrying a brand new set of bagpipes.

The goose thrust the bagpipes into Shane's hands. Then it pushed the golden table out of the way with its wings.

All the banshees cheered, and turned to look at Shane.

Shane's heart was beating fast, but there was only one thing he could do. He picked up the bagpipes, took a deep breath and started to play. To his astonishment, a fantastic tune came tumbling from the pipes! In fact, it was the best tune he had heard in his whole life.

He couldn't believe he was really playing it!

The banshees loved it. They lifted up their long skirts and started to dance.

Shane played the pipes for hours and hours. It was the easiest thing in the world. He played hundreds of different tunes. Each one sounded just as fantastic as the first.

The banshees had a wild time. They danced and floated around Shane like pale grey ghosts, and they wailed in time with the music. They even blew him kisses.

Shane had never been so popular. It was the best party he had ever been to.

At last, the goose came back, flapping
its wings. It told Shane the party was over.
The banshees all stopped dancing, and
clapped loudly. Then
one by one,
they went up
to Shane,
and each
pressed a
golden coin
into his hand.

Soon Shane had so many coins that he
couldn't hold them, and they spilled all over
the floor. So the goose brought him a big
sack, and Shane dropped all the money into it.
Yes! He was rich!

The pooka came back and started butting Shane again. "Come on Shane, my old lad!" it said. "It's time to go home."

So Shane jumped on the pooka's back, and the pooka galloped out of the rock, down the mountain, across the misty marshes and windy hills. The sun rose: it was already daybreak.

At last, they got back to the bridge near Shane's house. There the pooka threw Shane off its back, and disappeared for ever.

Shane ran straight into his house.

"Mum, Mum!" he shouted. "I've just ridden a pooka and met some banshees. Come and see what I've brought home!"

"Och, what's this nonsense you're blabbering on about?" scolded his mother.

"It's not nonsense!" cried Shane. "They gave me some new bagpipes and listen, I can play them properly now."

He showed her his beautiful new set of pipes. Then he tried to play them. But he couldn't get a single tune out of them. They made a horrible, rasping sound – like a honking goose.

Shane turned red with shame. He threw the bagpipes to the floor and fetched the sack he'd carried home from the banshees' party.

"Look," he said, "the banshees gave me all this gold!"

He tipped the sack upside down. But no gold fell out of it. There was nothing in it except dead leaves.

Shane's mother was angry with him for telling lies.
She sent him straight to his room, and there was no supper for him that night.

Shane felt terrible. Maybe it was true what people said about him: he was totally useless.

The next morning,
Shane crept sadly out
of the house. He had his
new set of pipes with him.
He planned to throw them into
the river.

He sat down on the bridge and looked at
the bagpipes. Maybe he would try and play
them just one last time. He picked them up,
took a deep breath . . .

. . . and a fantastic tune came out!

It was just like at the banshees' party! He played tune after tune without stopping, and each one was even better than the last.

Soon, a great crowd had come to the bridge to listen. They stared at Shane with goggle eyes. Was this really useless young Shane? He'd suddenly turned into the best piper in all Ireland!

From that day on, Shane never lost his gift for music. He loved to play his pipes, and no one ever called him useless again.